CW00508164

A time chart for Farnham: How people earned their living, when buildings were built, major events and prominent people.

	1100	1200	1300	1400	1500	1600	1700	1800	1900	2000
Royal House	Normans	Plantagenets		Lancaster / York	Tudors	Stuarts		Hanoverians	Windsor	
Earning a Living		Wheat, Wool and Cloth					Hops and Brewing		Service Industry	
Building	Farnham Castle	St. Andrew's / The Borough	Waverley Abbey			The Corn Market	Georgian Age		Farnham Grows	
Events	1 / 2 / 3		4 / 5 / 6	7 / 8 / 9		10 / 11 / 12	13	14 / 15 / 16	17 / 18	19
People	Henry of Blois		William of Wykeham			George Morley		William Cobbett		

KEY to events: 1 - French Invasion. 2 - The Borough Charter. 3 - Commutation of bond service. 4 - The Black Death. 5 - Westminster Hall R[e...]. 6 - Old Vicarage built. 7 - Wayneflete's Tower. 8 - Prince Arthur at Farnham Castle. 9 - Waverley Abbey closed. 10 - Windsor Houses. 11 - Civil War. 12 - Execution of Charles I. 13 - No. 10 Castle Street built. 14 - Farnham Gas Company. 15 - Farnham Station. 16 - Aldershot home of the British Army. 17 - John Henry Knight's motor car. 18 - Two World Wars. 19 - Bypass com[...]

Published 2021 by

The Farnham and District Museum Society

Typeset by the author

This book was originally published in 2021 by the Farnham and District Museum Society under ISBN 978-0-901638-33-5

Printed and bound by Print2Demand Ltd, Westoning.

A SHORT HISTORY OF FARNHAM

Roy Waight

FARNHAM AND DISTRICT MUSEUM SOCIETY

CONTENTS

Farnham is rich in history. Several fine books have been written about it. However, there isn't currently available a short book, aimed at students, which describes the whole history of Farnham. This book seeks to provide that. It is based on material available in the Farnham Museum Library. It uses the many papers published by the Farnham and District Museum Society.

It is arranged chronologically. Each chapter deals with a different period. At the end of each chapter, there are a few questions. Readers might like to use them as prompts to explore their town. Further reading is suggested for those particularly interested in the contents of the chapter.

It begins with an overall timeline of Farnham's history. It includes two maps which show some of the places mentioned in the text.

The Farnham and District Museum Society exists to investigate the history of Farnham and surrounding district. It seeks to promote interest in Farnham's history. It welcomes anyone who wishes to learn more. More particularly, it welcomes anyone who wishes to join, and become a part of the long endeavour to learn more about the long history of our town and district.

Introduction

1

Long before there was a town here, people have lived in the area around Farnham. They came and went with the weather. Ten thousand years ago, the whole area was cold and icy. This was the last ice age and it was far too cold for people to live here. But as the weather warmed up and the ice retreated, people moved into the area. They came from the mainland of Europe which, at that time, was connected to England. These people we call Mesolithic people, and they hunted animals and gathered berries. They settled in camps on high ground or where there was a supply of fresh water from a spring. There were no villages, but they made camps. They would wander off looking for animals to hunt but would often return to the camp. One such camp, where these men made their stone tools called flints, was discovered a hundred years ago. It is by the side of the sewage works on Monkton Lane. All you can see now is a stone memorial. The words are rather difficult to read.

About six thousand years ago, people learned to farm the land and domesticate animals like cattle and sheep. We call these people Neolithic. They made settlements which were bigger than before, and each settlement was surrounded by a ditch. They still used stone tools. They made large burial mounds called long barrows. Not far from the Mesolithic flint-knapping settlement, you can find the remains of a

Neolithic long barrow. It is just east of the industrial estate at Badshot Lea.

Later still, perhaps three thousand years ago, people learnt how to use metal. First of all bronze and, then, best of all, iron. Tools made with iron were better than tools made with stone and these iron age men cleared forest and built forts. Their farming provided them with more food than hunting did, and the population increased. We don't know much about the history of the area around Farnham at this time, but we know that these people belonged to tribes, each ruled by a chief. They worshipped pagan gods and built temples. We know, too, that they traded goods over long distances.

Some of the tracks that still exist today were started by these iron age people. Two of them, one running from Cornwall in the west to Dover in the east, and another running north and south, met around what is now Farnham. Maybe the north-south track crossed the River Wey at Longbridge. If you go there today, you can see what may be the oldest artefact in Farnham. The old sarsen stone might mark the best place to cross the river and is more than three thousand years old.

These iron age people are sometimes called Celts. They also traded with the Celts who lived across the English Channel. They were warlike people and the Romans had conquered them not long before. The Romans decided that they would conquer the Celts in England, too. They invaded in 43 AD and soon the whole of England was ruled by the Romans. They

Above: The old sarsen stone by Longbridge.

stayed for nearly four hundred years. People soon started to copy Roman behaviour. The better off Celts, Britons as we also call them, learnt to read and write. Towards the end of the Romans' stay in England, the first Christians arrived in England.

We don't know how the area around Farnham looked in Roman times, but we have some clues. The Romans were great builders. They constructed roads and impressive country houses called villas. Villas have been found near Farnham but there is no evidence that the Romans built a town at Farnham itself. The nearest town seems to have been at Holybourne, near Neatham. However, we know that they did build a pottery here.

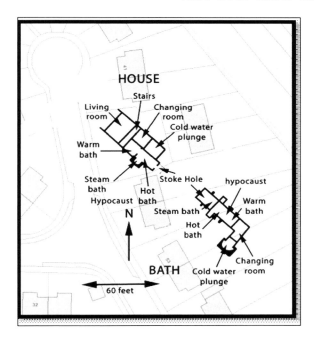

If you go to Roman Way you can see a plaque on a house wall where, a hundred years ago archaeologists discovered a bathhouse and residence which were part of a Roman pottery. In Farnham Park, archaeologists discovered a pottery kiln which formed part of the pottery. Water was taken from the Park to the bathhouse by an aqueduct.

By and large, the area around Farnham prospered in Roman times and the population increased. Most people worked on the land, maybe for the Roman rulers who lived in their villas. The area around Farnham was quite fertile and provided plenty of food. In the forest we now call Alice Holt, the Romans

Above: The plan of the Roman buildings discovered where Roman Way is today.

found clay and they soon started making pottery and bricks there.

See if you can:

• Find where the Roman bath and house were discovered.

• Find the stone marking the location of the Mesolithic settlement near Monkton Lane.

• Find the remains of the long barrow at Badshot Lea.

Further reading:

Hidden Depths – An archaeological Exploration of Surrey's Past, by Roger Hunt, David Graham, Giles Pattison & Rob Poulton. Publ. Surrey Archaeological Society, 2002.

2

In 410 AD, the Romans left England to return to defend Rome against invaders. The area around Farnham, like the rest of England, was left undefended. Soon people we call Anglo-Saxons arrived from what is now Denmark and Germany. They, too, were warlike and had no interest in Roman villas and the comfortable life of a Roman. They were pagans, worshipping savage gods. There was much conflict. Villas decayed and Roman towns were abandoned. For a couple of hundred years, history was a confused picture of warring tribes and petty kings. But slowly some kind of order returned. St. Augustine of Canterbury arrived in 599 AD and set about trying to turn the local kings into Christians. He had considerable success. The organisation of the church provided a model which the kings began to adopt. Many of them became Christian. The dozens of little kingdoms which had been fighting each other for a couple of centuries started to join into larger

Above: The first of three reliefs on the side of Hawthorn Lodge shows key elements of Saxon and medieval Farnham: Bishop, knight, deer, hunting dog, corn and a battlement.

kingdoms. The larger kingdom which came to dominate in the Farnham area was the kingdom of Wessex. It was with a king of Wessex, King Caedwalla, that the history of Farnham as a place with a name begins.

King Caedwalla was a fierce warrior. He started out as a pagan. He was quite willing to kill people. He did

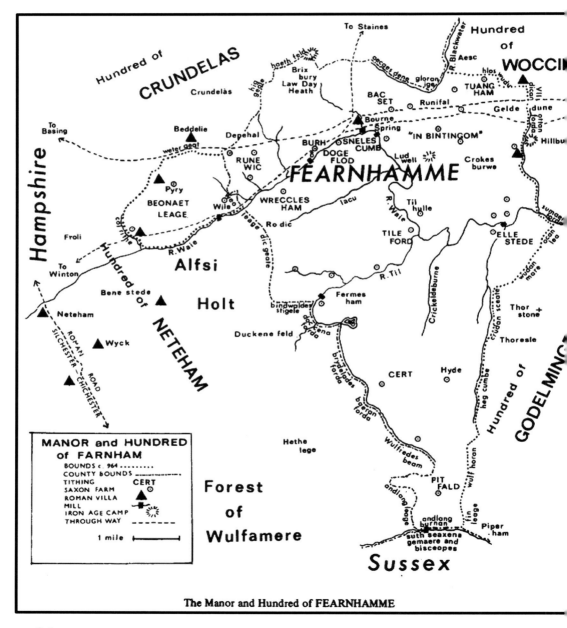

The Manor and Hundred of FEARNHAMME

not live long but towards the end of his life he was converted to Christianity by a courageous Christian called St. Wilfred. Perhaps seeking forgiveness for his sins, King Caedwalla started giving away land to the church. In the year 688 he gave 'Fearnham' to the church and asked them to build what was called a minster, or church. He wanted all the people who lived in the Farnham area to become Christian. The 'Fearnham' which he gave was much, much larger than what we call Farnham today. It covered all the land between Aldershot and Churt, Bentley and Elstead.

In Saxon times the land was organised into manors which were owned by lords of the manor. Administration of the country was through county courts, or what were called shire courts. Counties were organised into 'hundreds'. The church was organised into dioceses ruled by a Bishop and these contained lots of parishes. The large area given to the church by King Caedwalla became in time, a manor, a parish, and a hundred. They all covered the same area.

We don't know if a minster was built straight away in Farnham, but we do know that there was already a settlement of Saxons in the Farnham area. If you go up Firgrove Hill, you can see a small close called Saxon Croft. Here archaeologists discovered a settlement of Saxon weavers' huts in 1924. The huts were there a hundred years before King Caedwalla. So it is likely that by the time Caedwalla was king there was some kind of Saxon settlement in Farnham. Historians believe it was probably located around where the church today is located.

To left: A map of the old Manor of Farnham and its surroundings in Saxon times, produced by local historian, Elfrida Manning.

Because there is little written evidence, we know little detail about how Saxon Farnham looked or how it was organised. We do know that within a hundred years of King Caedwalla, the Manor of Farnham was owned by the Bishop of Winchester. We also know that things were not always peaceful. The area was often attacked by the Vikings who had started invading England from about 800 AD. There was a famous 'Battle of Farnham' in 893 AD when the Vikings were defeated by King Edward the Elder. There is a legend that Farnham itself was defended by the women of Farnham who occupied and defended the church tower.

See if you can:

• Find where the Saxon weavers' huts were found.

• Find the old Saxon centre of Farnham and think why the first settlers might have chosen this spot.

• See how many of the Saxon names included in the map have survived, with changed spelling, to this day.

Further reading:

Saxon Farnham by Elfrida Manning, publ. by Phillimore, 1970.

3

History becomes clearer after William the Conqueror arrived in 1066. After defeating King Harold at The Battle of Hastings, William made his way to London to seize the throne. He may have passed through Farnham on his way there. We are not sure. William quickly stole all the land of England and gave it to his Norman followers. We know so much about Farnham at that time because King William got his men to record who owned what. The Manor of Farnham stayed the property of the Bishop of Winchester, though the Saxon bishop was kicked out and replaced by a Norman.

The Domesday Book reveals that the Manor of Farnham contained in total only about 500 people. There were several slaves. There were three 'free men'. The rest were peasants. Most would have been busy farming the surrounding land, even if a group of them actually lived in a settlement in Farnham. However, there were others who even at the time of the Norman Conquest possessed special status. The miller was one. There were several mills in Farnham Manor. They included a mill at Bourne Mill, another

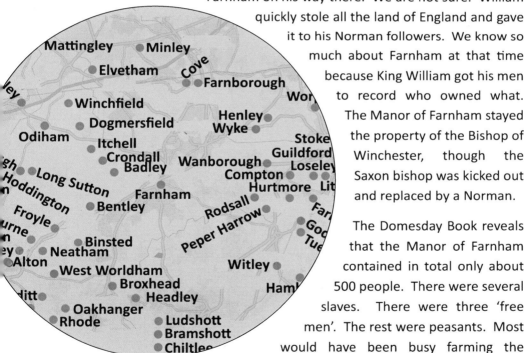

Above: This shows part of a map of the various manors at the time of Domesday within a twelve mile radius of Farnham, centred on Farnham.

at Hatch Mill and another at Weydon, the Medmulle. Mills were enormously important because people had to bring their corn to the mill. The system William introduced, with peasants and noblemen, we call feudalism.

King William's invasion was followed by a couple of hundred years when the population grew strongly and more and more land was cultivated. It was also the time when three great building projects were completed. These were to be important to the history of Farnham.

To right: An artist's impression of the Great Hall at Farnham Castle when it was first built (courtesy of English Heritage).

First, in 1128, an abbey was established at Waverley, just two miles south of Farnham. The monks of the Abbey wore a white habit. They belonged to an important order of monks called the Cistercians. This was the first Cistercian Abbey in England. Over the next two hundred years this grew into a large monastery with a great church as big as a cathedral. This was important because it brought lots of skilled people into the area who were good

To left: An artist's impression of how Waverley Abbey might have looked after the completion of the great Priory Church of St. Mary (courtesy of Historic England).

farmers, skilled in raising sheep. The wool and cloth they produced brought wealth to the area. A little later, the great bishop, Henry of Blois, brother of King Stephen, built a keep at Farnham, which became Farnham Castle.

Henry of Blois built several castles. This is one of the few that survives. These were troubled times. When King Henry I died, he wanted his daughter, Matilda, to become Queen. The barons, instead, wanted King Stephen to be King. For twenty years King and Queen fought each other. This may well explain why Henry built a castle in Farnham.

r court in the Great Hall

This soon grew to include a Bishop's Palace below the Keep. And at about the same time, today's church of St. Andrew's was started. It probably replaced the earlier Saxon minster. People who lived in the countryside around Farnham had to walk miles to get to church. All this building work had to be done by somebody. Many of the local peasants would have spent an enormous amount of time labouring away. But many more would have been brought in from elsewhere. Farnham, just a small settlement at the time of the Norman Conquest, was soon the location of two great buildings: Farnham Castle and the Church of St. Andrew's; and just a couple of miles away, the Abbey of Waverley. It was suddenly an important place.

The Abbot of Waverley and the Bishop of Winchester were usually close friends. The Bishop had many palaces to stay in but, when he came to Farnham, he would see the Abbot and some of his more important

To left: The ruined keep and the Bishop's Palace at Farnham Castle.

monks. You can imagine a line of monks in their white robes making their way along Waverley Lane, along Abbey Street, up what is now Bear Lane, to the Castle to see the Bishop. They would have looked like a procession of enormous pigeons.

One further thing of great importance to Farnham dates from this time, namely the Borough. You must realise that when William invaded England, Farnham was not a town, just a small cluster of cottages around the Saxon minster church. We might describe it as a Saxon hamlet. But the same bishop who built the Castle, Henry of Blois, was keen to develop a new settlement north of Saxon Farnham on higher ground and protected by his new Castle. It was probably Henry of Blois who created what became known as the Borough at about the time he built his Castle. This was basically a new town, although maybe the word 'town' is a bit too grand. It was built on either side of a wide street, what we today call Castle Street. It extended down to the road at right angles to it, which we still call The Borough.

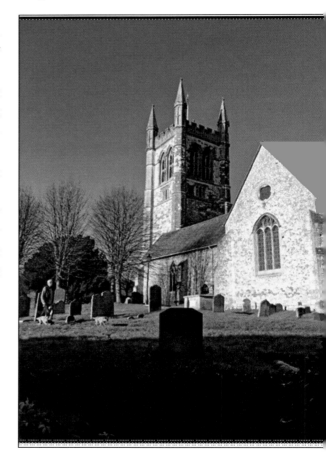

This new town was defended by a large ditch, thirty feet across and twelve feet deep. It had entrances and people coming into the new town had to pass through these gates. Now this was a time when the economy was growing rapidly. Kings of England were keen to see the country become wealthier. So they

Above: The Church of St. Andrew has seen many modifications and enlargements but originated in the twelfth century.

started granting charters to places like Farnham which gave them the right to organise a market. And this is what happened at Farnham. A market soon developed. King John granted a charter. The market was held each week, and people bringing goods to market had to pay a toll when they entered the Borough. Farnham soon became an important local marketplace used by anyone from miles around wanting to buy or sell things.

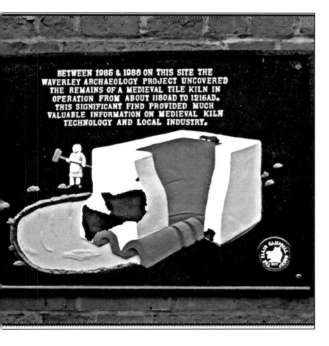

Above: In Borelli's Yard you can see a plaque commemorating the discovery of an old medieval kiln. The town ditch surrounding the Borough ran nearby.

Then, in 1258, Bishop William Raleigh granted to the Borough what remains its proudest possession, a charter which made the Borough largely independent. From then on, the Borough, ruled by its own burgesses, was largely independent of the Bishop. Of course, the Bishop demanded payment for granting this privilege; £12 a year. That doesn't sound much, but a pound was worth much more then than it is today. £1 a year was a reasonable wage for a labourer in 1258.

King John was not the only King who visited Farnham. Because Farnham had an important Bishop's Palace up at the Castle, it was visited by most of the kings and queens of England. King John, like several others, came to hunt deer in the Great Park which stretched from Farnham all the way to Windsor. When a King arrived he brought with him an enormous group of people: soldiers, scribes and noblemen as well as everything he needed to hold court. King Henry VIII and Queen Elizabeth I both visited Farnham several times. They carried out business at the Castle and then relaxed by hunting. The Bishops, too, were keen on hunting. People who poached deer from the Park were punished or fined.

King James I so loved Farnham Castle that for a while he leased it from the Bishop. A fire broke out on one occasion when the King was staying. He wasn't hurt but several of his horses were burned to death.

See if you can:

• Find the arrow slits in the keep at Farnham Castle.

• Find the remains of the Chapter House at Waverley Abbey.

• Identify which parts of St. Andrew's church date from Norman times.

• Find where the ditch ran in Borelli's Yard.

Further reading:

A Convenient Place - a History of Farnham Castle, by R D Waight, publ. by the Farnham and District Museum Society, 2020.

The White Monks of Waverley, by G. Ware, publ. by the Farnham and District Museum Society, 1976.

4

By this time, Farnham and its Castle had already seen some excitement. King John had fallen out with his followers, the barons who, with the Church, owned

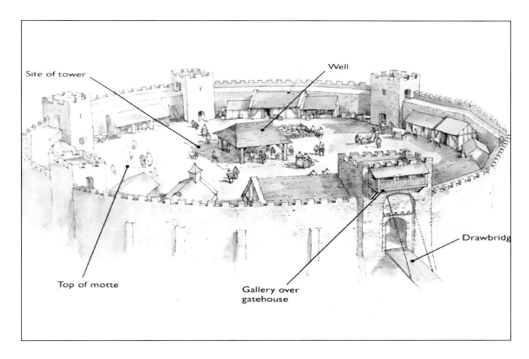

Site of tower

Well

Drawbridg

Top of motte

Gallery over
gatehouse

most of England. He was forced to sign the famous Magna Carta at Runnymede in 1215. This guaranteed certain basic rights; that all men should be subject to fair trial, for example. The King was unhappy with being forced to sign such a document and he discussed what he should do with his close associate, Bishop Peter des Roches, up at Farnham Castle. In

Above: An artist's impression of how the Farnham Castle keep might have looked in about 1350 (Courtesy of English Heritage).

1216, King John changed his mind and rejected the Charter he had recently sigtned. The barons were so angry that they invited the French King to invade England. And they did.

For the last time, England was invaded. Farnham Castle was taken by the French without a struggle.

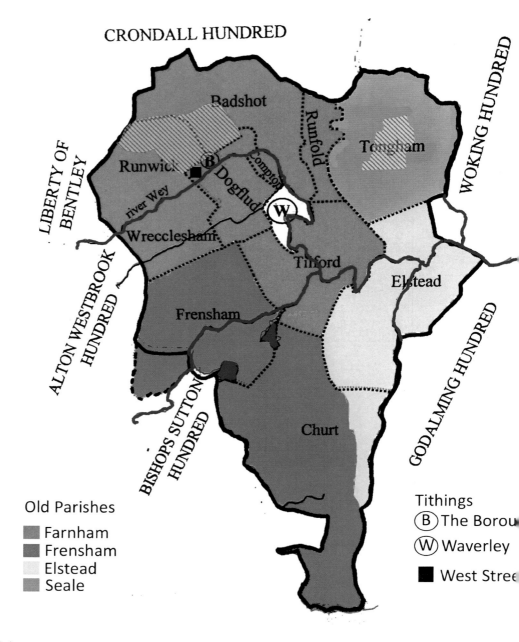

CRONDALL HUNDRED

Old Parishes

■ Farnham
■ Frensham
■ Elstead
■ Seale

Tithings
(B) The Borou
(W) Waverley
■ West Stree

For a year they held the Castle. The French soldiers did great damage to the surrounding area as they stole food and vandalised property. When King John died late in 1216, the barons decided they had made a mistake inviting the French King to invade. The great knight, William Marshall, helped by the Bishop, Peter des Roches, managed to kick the French out and Farnham Castle was returned to the Bishop.

Whether any of these arguments between barons and kings would have affected the residents of the Manor of Farnham very much is difficult to say. Obviously, they would have been affected by the vandalism of the French soldiers but, otherwise, what went on had little effect on them. What did it matter to a peasant farming the land if one French-speaking nobleman or bishop was replaced by another French-speaking nobleman or bishop? He would never have met either anyway. And the land had to be farmed, always, or starvation threatened. There was no supermarket to go to. He just had to get on with things.

Farnham Castle has not seen a great deal of fighting. Farnham has been mostly a peaceful place. There was great trouble during the period when the Castle was built, when King Stephen of Blois and Empress Matilda fought each other for nearly twenty years in what was called 'The Great Anarchy'. And as just described, there was the French invasion and occupation. But during the Second Baron's War, when Simon de Montfort briefly ruled England in place of the King, Henry III, Farnham escaped damage. The Bishop up at the Castle was a supporter of Simon, who occupied the neighbouring castle at Odiham.

The Bishop also took good care to develop inside the Castle Keep a palace with a hall, chapel, barracks,

To left: The map shows the old Hundred of Farnham as it was at the end of the Middle Ages. The four parishes are shown in colour, the various tithings are named. The Borough is indicated as is Waverley, which was not part of a parish. The hatched areas are the Bishop's demesne, the farmland he farmed for his own account.

armoury, store rooms, as well as pens for sheep and coops for chickens.   He was taking no chances.

See if you can:

• Find the hole through which soldiers defending the keep at Farnham Castle poured boiling oil on to the attackers below.

Further reading:

A Convenient Place - a History of Farnham Castle, by R D Waight, publ. by the Farnham and District Museum Society, 2020.

5

How did ordinary people live in the Manor of Farnham at this time? The usual answer is 'feudalism'. Feudalism lasted from the time of William the Conqueror and gradually died out by the time the Tudor Age arrived. Basically, the King owned everything 'by right of conquest'. His most important supporters, Norman noblemen who had helped him win the Battle of Hastings, or important bishops, were given manors. They enjoyed the income of these manors in return for giving the king their support. This support meant providing the king with an agreed number of knights who could fight for the king when necessary. The Bishop of Winchester, who was incredibly rich, had some sixty manors! Farnham Manor was only one of them.

Above: The timeless rhythm of the countryside. Cutting hay with scythes.

As far as a common man was concerned, the important figure was the lord of the manor. The Bishop of Winchester was the lord of the manor of Farnham. However, Farnham didn't see much of the Bishop; he was far too busy. He was not only an important churchman. Most of the bishops were also important politicians and officials of the King. The Bishop's work in Farnham was conducted for him by his steward and other officials. The reeve was one of these and particularly important. Almost all the people in the Manor were peasants. Unless they were 'freemen' (and they were not many) they were 'bond men' and 'bond women'. Just as the lord of the manor gave knight service to the king in return for his manor, the bonded peasant gave 'bond service' to the lord of the manor in return for the use of an amount of land.

Most bonded peasants held either a 'virgate' of land (about 30 acres) or a 'half-virgate' (about 15 acres). People called cottars held perhaps two or three acres. A virgate provided enough food to feed a family with sometimes a surplus. Two or three acres weren't enough, and cottars had to work for other peasants to make ends meet. Slaves owned no land. However, slaves mostly became cottars by being given some land. Slavery died out quickly. There were no slaves by 1100. The bonded peasant worked his land to provide food for his family, sold any surplus in the market, and did work for his lord free of charge. He would work on the lord's own farmland, known as the 'demesne'. He would provide eggs or honey. He would cart firewood to the Castle. He would mend fences. And he would pay rent for the land he cultivated.

Above: When the Bishop or the King arrived in Farnham, the kitchen at The Castle would have been very busy with a hundred men or more to feed (courtesy English Heritage).

It is difficult to appreciate this model when you live in modern Farnham. The lord of the manor did not own you, like a slave, but you were tied to the land. His rule was law. You couldn't leave the land without his permission. You could not marry off your daughter without his permission and the payment of a fine. Everything you did with your land was subject to the manor court. It was like Russia under serfdom. On the other hand, if you obeyed the law and the customs, you were mostly left in peace.

However, there was a chink in this model of absolute servitude. The Borough! As a contemporary writer said, 'the town makes you free'. The men of the Borough managed their own affairs as long as they paid the lord of the manor their £12 yearly fee. And the idea that people might be allowed to escape bondage in return for an annual payment was attractive, not only to the peasant, who resented having to do unpaid work for his lord, but by the lord himself, who didn't always find getting his bondmen to work easy. The bishop who followed Bishop Raleigh, a violent young man called Aymer de Valence, decided to exchange the bond work of his peasants for an annual payment.

This he did in 1256. For the princely sum of £27 a year he excused his peasants of most of their 'bond service'. Individual acts of 'commutation' as this was called had happened before. This was the first wholesale 'commutation' of bond service in the Bishop's many manors. Just a year after the Borough had taken a step towards independence, the whole of the bonded peasants enjoyed a great increase in liberty. The model of feudalism was breaking down. Relationships between the lord of the manor and his peasants had been relationships of bond service. They were becoming money relationships.

Of course, the bishop, lord of the manor as well as one of the most important of the bishops, remained enormously important. His importance was all the greater because he was usually not only a bishop, but holder of high office as well. Nine of the bishops of Winchester became chancellors of England. This position, chancellor, was comparable with that of the prime minister today. It would not be until the age of Henry VIII and the Tudors that the importance of the Bishop would suddenly decline. The power and authority of these extraordinary men is difficult to appreciate these days. But we have much to thank them for. By and large, they administered efficiently, judged fairly, and kept the peace.

See if you can:

• Find where in Farnham Castle all the bishops of Winchester who were also chancellors of England are pictured in stained glass.

• Discover which two Bishops of Winchester were also made cardinals.

Further reading:

A Convenient Place - a History of Farnham Castle, by R D Waight, publ. by the Farnham and District Museum Society, 2020.

Above: Various Bishops of Winchester as portrayed in plaster in the small Museum at Farnham Castle: from top left - Frank Theodore Woods, Richard Fox, Lancelot Andrewes,

William Wayneflete, George
Morley, John Thomas,
Charles Sumner and Stephen
Gardiner. The Bishops of
Winchester were the lords
of the Manor of Farnham as
well as bishops.

50 Places to see in Central Farnham

1	Farnham Castle Keep	26	Site of old gasworks
2	The Bishop's Palace	27	U.C.A.
3	Fox's Steps	28	The Hart
4	Farnham Park	29	Timber Close
5	Guildford House	30	Lion and Lamb Yard
6	The Avenue	31	Malthouse Yard
7	Bear Lane	32	Bethune House
8	Loundes Passage	33	65A West Street
9	The Nelson Arms	34	Wilmer House
10	Park Row	35	Timber Hall
11	The Windsor Alms Houses	36	Vernon House
12	Zizzi's	37	The Old Grammar School
13	2 Minutes Silence	38	The Bishop's Table
14	10 Castle Street	39	Cat's paw mark
15	Decorated downpipes	40	Cobbett's Tomb
16	The Bailiffs' Hall	41	St. Andrew's
17	The Hop Blossom	42	The Old Vicarage
18	40 The Borough	43	Blind, and bricked-in, windows
19	Borelli's Yard	44	Waggon Yard
20	The Bush	45	The Maltings
21	The Woolmead	46	Red Lion Lane
22	Old Corset Factory	47	Tanyard House
23	The Spire Church	48	The Sarsen Stone
24	Victoria Gardens	49	The William Cobbett
25	Wheelwright's Shop	50	Farnham Station

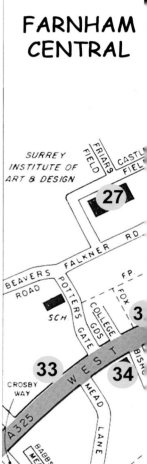

FARNHAM CENTRAL

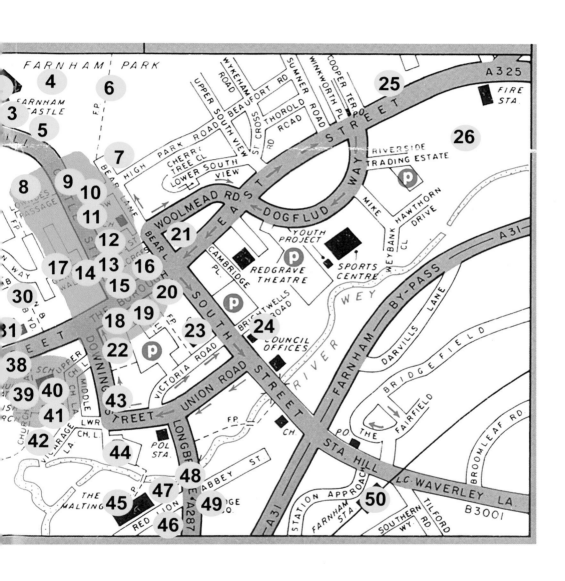

PLACES TO SE[

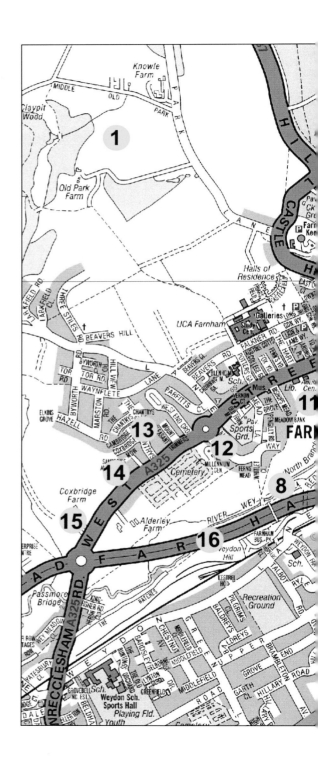

1   Old Park
2   Roman buildings
3   Mesolithic site
4   Long Barrow
5   Waverley
6   Bourne Mill
7   Hatch Mill
8   Weydon Mill
9   Shepherd & Flock
10   Saxon Croft
11   Marquis of Lothian's Walk
12   Crosby's Way
13   The Chantrys
14   Sampson's Alms-house
15   Coxbridge Farm
16   The Bypass
17   Great Austins

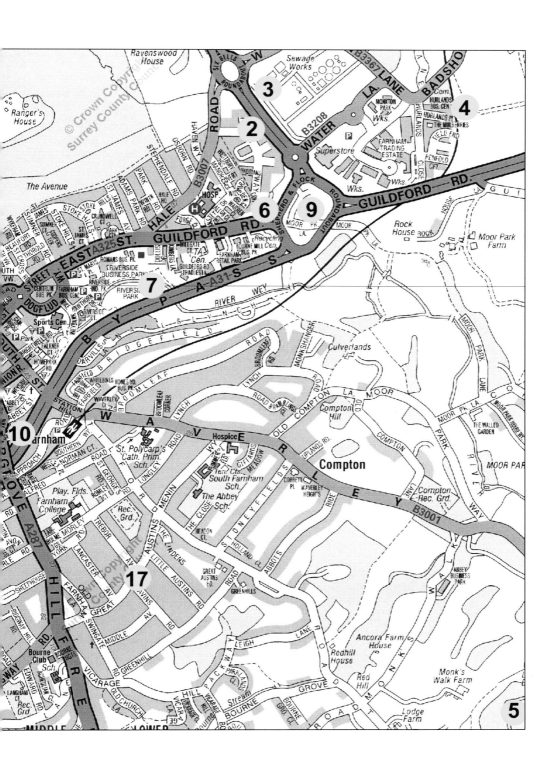

To right: The great hammer-beam roof of Westminster Hall, constructed at Farnham and floated down the Thames to London.

6

The fourteenth century was a terrible time for Farnham. It started with a great famine; the worst northern Europe had experienced since records began. Then in 1348 came the Black Death. Half the population of the Manor of Farnham died within two years. As a result, things changed utterly and yet things seemed at first not to change.

The Manor of Farnham continued to operate as before with remarkably little disruption. Indeed, within half a century Farnham was able to make its greatest contribution to Western art. This came about when Richard II decided he wanted to rebuild Westminster Hall in London. This had been built originally by William II. Now Richard wanted a new building and, most difficult, a new roof. This would have to be the biggest wooden structure in Europe. To supervise its building, he turned to the Bishop of Winchester, the great William of Wykeham. William had supervised other building projects. He was close to the great carpenter, Hugh Herland, the king's master carpenter.

And so Farnham became the place where the greatest wooden structure in the history of Europe was assembled. It took a couple of years to build. Then the mighty roof was disassembled and floated own the River Thames to Westminster Hall where it was

Above: The Old Vicarage ... perhaps the oldest residence in Farnham, dated to 1417.

reassembled. It can still be seen today. Nobody knows for sure where in Farnham the roof was made. The plaque on Lion and Lamb Way states that it was constructed on Timber Close. Others think it more likely that it was constructed at the Castle. It is at any rate a masterpiece and many are not aware it was made in Farnham. It is as if the residents of Florence knew nothing of Michelangelo's David.

Below: Tanyard House, another old and picturesque building, dating from early Tudor times.

With the population halved and much land gone to waste, William of Wykeham decided in 1376 to enclose the land to the east of his Castle and thereby created what is now Farnham Park. When you walk around the Park you can think of the great bishop. Not everything there, of course, dates back to William of Wykeham.

The Avenue and the Ranger's House are much later. But all of these owe their existence to different bishops of Winchester and we may award them a nod of thanks.

But in the long run, the Black Death changed things utterly. With the population of labourers halved, there were too few people to till the soil. Landlords like the lord of the manor couldn't find people to rent their lands. Rents went down. The scarcity of labour meant that wages went up. For the first time in three hundred years, the peasants become much better off. Moreover, there were so many empty plots that the most enterprising of the peasants took over vacant plots and larger farms started to emerge. What is known as the yeoman farmer enterred onto the scene.

In time, the population stabilised. Many cottages had fallen into disrepair but, at the beginning of the fifteenth century, people started again to build houses. It is from this period that the oldest residences in Farnham survive. The Old Vicarage dates from 1417. The old Timber Hall beside the library on West Street may be even older and have housed the carpenters working on the Westminster Hall roof. Tanyard House dates from a century later, though it looks older than

Above: Images of death and destruction were common in medieval times. Here are the Four Horsemen of the Apocalypse: Pestilence, War, Famine, and Death.

that. Many of the modern facades of Farnham houses hide old houses dating back to these years. The ironstone central gutter of lower Church Street gives an idea of how medieval Farnham might have looked though it, too, is later.

See if you can:

• Locate where the great Westminster Hall Roof was assembled in Farnham.

• Find The Old Vicarage.

• Find Tanyard House.

• Find any other buildings in Farnham that were built before 1500.

• Walk round Farnham Park and see if you can see any deer.

Further reading:

Mediaeval Farnham: Everyday Life in an Episcopal Manor, by E. Robo, publ. by E W Langham, Farnham, 1935.

The History of Farnham Park, by Pat Heather, publ. by the Farnham and District Museum Society in collaboration with Waverley Borough Council, 2009

Henry VII became king in 1485 and ushered in the Tudor Age. A few years before, in 1475, another great bishop, William of Wayneflete, built the magnificent tower that is often called Fox's Tower. Although not Tudor, it looks Tudor. It is Farnham's finest building. The Bishop was followed by Richard Fox, Farnham's best-known bishop, who some say built the steps leading to Farnham Castle: seven steps and seven paces repeated. Bishop Fox was blind, and the regularity of the steps made it easier for him to descend them. There followed a century of drama which changed Farnham, and England, completely.

Above: A model of the Old Market House built in 1566. It used to stand at the bottom of Castle Street. Sadly, it was demolished in the nineteenth century (courtesy of the Farnham and District Museum Society).

It began with one of those rare occasions when Farnham stepped to the front of the stage of England's long history. Henry VII was worried that his son, Prince Arthur, was a little fragile. Because the air in Farnham was healthy, he asked the Bishop to look after his son. So Arthur spent his first few years at Farnham Castle. The air proved healthy, and the

prince flourished. He was married to Catherine of Aragon at the age of 14. Sadly, shortly afterwards, he caught a sickness and died. His brother, Henry VIII, went on to marry Catherine in his turn. They were happy but she was not able to give him the son he wanted. He divorced her and went on to marry five more wives. The rest is history.

Above: William of Wayneflete built the magnificent tower known as Fox's Tower in 1475.

Because the Pope would not agree to divorce Henry from Catherine, he made himself head of the Church in England. In the debate that followed, he rejected the Pope's authority and made England a protestant country. This was called the Reformation. It ushered in a century or more of religious argument between Protestants and Catholics. Henry also decided to get rid of the monasteries and seize their wealth.

As a result, Waverley Abbey was seized and given away to one of Henry's cronies. It was soon falling apart as men stole the stones to make other buildings. Under Henry VIII, so much changed. For one thing, the bishops lost their political power. They had always been powerful men who helped run the country. They were statesmen as well as churchmen. After Henry, none of the bishops ever again helped rule the country. They simply became bishops. After Henry died, his protestant son Edward became King. The protestants were delighted. Then Edward died and his Catholic daughter, Mary, became Queen. The Catholics were delighted. The new bishop, John White, was a Catholic and was actually born in Farnham, the only Bishop of Winchester to be a son of Farnham. Unfortunately for him, after Mary died, Elizabeth I became Queen and things swung back to the protestants again. John White was imprisoned and died soon after.

Elizabeth I also changed many things. Farnham was by now a growing town but not everyone did well. Once, everyone had enjoyed the product of some land. After the Black Death, those peasants remaining alive had taken over vacant land and, as the population increased again, more and more people were landless. Poverty became a big problem for Elizabeth. She gave responsibility for looking after the poor to the local church, what was called 'The

Vestry'. The importance of the lord of the manor began to fade away.

See if you can:

- Find the Tudor wing of Farnham Castle.

- Decide why the Tower at Farnham Castle built by Bishop William of Wayneflete is called Fox's Tower.

- Decide if you believe that Fox's Steps were made the way they were to help the blind Bishop Fox go up and down them.

Further reading:

The Reformation and its effects on Farnham, by the Rt. Revd. Christopher Herbert, publ. by the Farnham and District Museum Society, 2020.

8

The people in Farnham had always made a living by farming and that remained true until recently. But after the Black Death, because of the shortage of labourers, more and more sheep were grazed on the land. Sheep did not need as much labour as growing crops. The wool was used to make cloth and the cloth

Below: The observant will notice how the corners of the buildings at the southern end of Downing Street are rounded so that the hundreds of wagons leaving Waggon Yard should not chip the brickwork.

market in Farnham became an important source of wealth.

Eventually fashions changed and the kind of cloth made in Farnham, called kersey, became unpopular. But as the cloth market faded away, a new market took its place, Farnham's Corn Market. During the seventeenth century, carrying corn by ship was dangerous because of the pirates who lurked in the Channel. The country was also in conflict at different times with France and Holland. They kept stealing cargoes. Instead, corn was brought to Farnham Market from the surrounding countryside, where the farmers sold it to dealers who then carried it overland to London. London was growing rapidly and needed to be fed. For a century or so, the corn market helped keep Farnham wealthy. Farms no longer cluster

Below: Waggon Yard is now a car park. Once it was home to hundreds of wagons on market days.

around the town of Farnham as they used to, though you can still see one at Coxbridge.

The name of the car park, Waggon Yard car park, reminds us of the great corn market in Farnham. On some days, a thousand wagons would come and go from the great Waggon Yard. The writer, Daniel Defoe, wrote in the early eighteenth century that he counted a thousand or so wagons coming into and going out of Waggon Yard. If you look carefully at the buildings at the bottom of Downing Street, you can see how the corners are rounded, so that passing waggons wouldn't chip them if they bumped into them.

Many of the corn traders in Farnham became wealthy. The owners of big farms also became wealthy and bought more and more land. But many were poor and landless. The division between the wealthy farmer and the poor labourer increased. The seventeenth century became an age of philanthropy, as rich men set up charities. An early example was Andrew Windsor, who made his money through the corn trade. In 1619, he built some beautiful alms-houses for poor people. The Windsor alms-houses are still there on Castle Street. Such acts have continued until today and Farnham has several alms-houses built by the wealthy.

See if you can:

• Find the wall plaque on the Windsor Alms-houses.

• Spot the rounded corners on the houses on Downing Street.

• See how many alms-houses there are in Farnham.

• Explain why the cloth trade declined in Farnham.

Further reading:

The Reformation and its effects on Farnham, by the Rt. Revd. Christopher Herbert, publ. by the Farnham and District Museum Society, 2020.

9

The Seventeenth Century was one of prosperity for many and poverty for even more. It was also torn in two by Civil War. The war was between the 'Roundheads' and the 'Cavaliers', the supporters of Parliament and the supporters of the King, Charles I. The Roundheads were eventually led by a great soldier, Oliver Cromwell. Farnham played an important role in the War. It was the headquarters of the parliamentary forces under a man called William Waller. The town was mostly sympathetic to the King. At first the Castle was occupied by Sir John Denham,

Below: Here Vernon House is depicted in watercolour by the artist J. Hassell. The date is 1822. The building is much changed and is now the town library, Charles II stayed here with his friend Henry Vernon on his way to execution in London.

but not for long. Interestingly, both William Waller and Sir John Denham were rather good poets.

The town only saw a little fighting. Most of the fighting was done elsewhere, at Basing House and in Alton. The troops stayed at Farnham Castle or local people were forced to put the soldiers up in their homes. Gallows were erected at the bottom of Castle Street where men were hanged if they were guilty of mutiny. The Castle was also used as a prison for captured prisoners. This was one of the unhappiest times for Farnham. Father fought son. Many soldiers

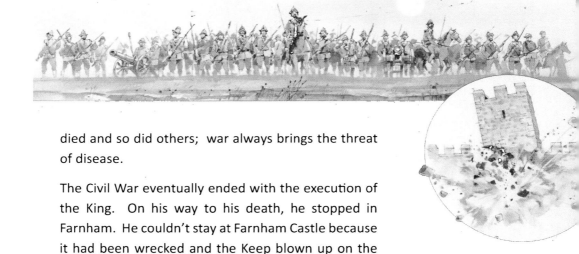

died and so did others; war always brings the threat of disease.

The Civil War eventually ended with the execution of the King. On his way to his death, he stopped in Farnham. He couldn't stay at Farnham Castle because it had been wrecked and the Keep blown up on the orders of Oliver Cromwell. So he stayed with an old and loyal friend, Henry Vernon, who lived at Vernon House. This is now the town library.

After the Restoration, when Charles II came back as king, something had to be done about the Castle which was almost in ruins. The new Bishop, George Morley, set about rebuilding the Palace. He didn't try to repair the Keep. What you see today is very much his work. He also helped establish the grammar school in Farnham. While he rebuilt the Bishop's Palace, his friend, Isaak Walton, lived there as his

Above: An artist's impression of the Civil War - soldiers on the attack and the blowing up of the Gatehouse at Farnham Castle (courtesy of English Heritage).

steward. Isaak Walton is famous today as the author of The Compleat Angler and several other books.

The Civil War did a lot of damage to Farnham, but people recovered quickly and soon the town was entering one of its richest periods.

See if you can:

• Find the Marquis of Lothian's Walk.

• Look at the 1822 picture of Vernon House as depicted by J. Hassell and see if you can tell which part of today's Vernon House corresponds to it.

Further reading:

Farnham in the Civil War and the Commonwealth, by L Spring & D Hall, publ. by The Farnham and District Museum Society, 2002.

The corn trade started to fade towards the end of the seventeenth century as sea transport became safer. But Farnham then discovered a new source of wealth: hops and brewing. Hops are used to preserve and give bight to beer. Farnham hops turned out to be the best. They could be sold at high prices at the market held each year at Weyhill. From the middle of the seventeenth century until around 1900, hops provided Farnham with great wealth. Not surprisingly, some of these wealthy men went on to set up breweries. They had corn, they had hops, and they could make beer. South of the River across from Waggon Yard, you can still see The Maltings, which was once a brewery. Later it became a Malting

Below: The wonderful old Maltings: tannery, malthouse, brewery and, most recently, arts and community centre.

House, where barley was turned into the mash used to make beer.

Since the Civil War ended, Farnham has enjoyed 350 years of relative peace. After the war was over, the residents of Farnham concentrated on the innocent business of making money. It seems as if almost everyone was growing hops. Hops were everywhere

Below: The hop bines carefully cast in the lead of the drain pipes on the corner of Caste Street and The Borough testify to the importance of hops to Farnham's prosperity in the 18th and 19th centuries.

in Farnham. The hop fields extended right up to the town on both the north and south of the River Wey. The Hart led into hop fields. Hop fields extended all the way to the Hop Blossom pub behind Castle Street.

Not everyone made money from hops. Hops are difficult to grow and you need to invest a lot of money in hop poles and the like before you can get a crop. A bad harvest meant that smaller hop growers went bankrupt. It was the richer hop growers who managed to survive a few bad years and they tended to buy up the hop fields of the bankrupt hop growers. As a result, hop growing in the end was dominated by a small number of wealthy farmers and hop growers. Famous Farnham families emerged through hops whose names are still remembered – for example the Knights, the Paines and the Trimmers. Although there are no longer any hop fields in Farnham, remnants of the golden years of hops remain.

Above: Malthouse Yard: one of many yards where hop-pickers brought their hops and received payment from the tally-man. The tiny window through which he dispensed cash is still there.

For example, the footpath which runs behind the Jolly Sailor pub marked the boundary of the hop fields on the north side of the town. The footpath is still there, though the hop fields have gone. In Malthouse Yard you can still see a tallyman's window where the hop pickers took their tally sticks and got paid. Perhaps the most beautiful house on West Street, Wilmer House, was built by a wealthy hop grower. Look carefully at the brickwork. It is superb.

Farnham from the Castle.

On the lead downpipes on the corner of Castle Street you can see the hop bines cast in relief, a celebration of the source of Farnham's wealth. On the wall of the Maltings facing Bridge Square you can still see, in faded paintwork, the name of one of Farnham's leading maltsters, a man with the unlikely name, Sampson Sampson.

One of the results of all this hop growing and brewing was that Farnham had lots of pubs. Some say Farnham had more pubs per head than any other town in England. Others say it also had the most ghosts. Maybe the two were connected! At the end of the nineteenth century Farnham had around a hundred pubs and beer houses. One of the most famous was The Jolly Farmer, which is still there, although now it is called The William Cobbett because the famous writer, William Cobbett, was born there. It sometimes seems as if half the buildings in Farnham were pubs at one time or another.

Above: An old postcard showing Farnham from the Castle. Look carefully and you can see how hopfields came right up to the buildings on Castle Street.

Farnham also has an unusual number of yards, usually found round the back of buildings. These yards were where many businesses were carried out. They were used for storage as well. There are more than two dozen off Castle Street, The Borough and West Street. Some are private, but others can be visited: St. George's Yard, Borelli's Yard, Fenn's Yard, Malthouse Yard and, of course, the Lion and Lamb Yard.

The age of hops was also an age of coaching with coaches travelling to London and elsewhere. People stopping at Farnham would stay at one of the many coaching inns in the town. The Bush Hotel, the most famous, is still there. Farnham buzzed with activity. West Street and Castle Street were where the wealthy lived. West Street was Farnham's West End. But there were poor parts of Farnham, too. Red Lion Lane was poor. Behind Castle Street, the servants who served the wealthy lived in tiny houses.

See if you can:

• Work out where the hop fields stopped north of West Street and west of Castle Street.

• Read something by William Cobbett.

• Find an old postcard showing the hop fields around Farnham.

Further reading:

Surrounded by Hops, The story of the Knight Family of Farnham, by Cathie Fitzgerald, publ. by the Farnham and District Museum Society, 2014.

11

Farnham is famous today for its wonderful Georgian buildings. The word 'Georgian' refers to the long period when England was ruled by Kings George numbers I, II, III and IV. These Georgian buildings were mostly built by wealthy hop growers. Castle Street, for example, is one of the finest Georgian streets in England. Not all the wonderful houses there were built during the reigns of the four Georges. Some were built a little earlier during the reign of Queen Anne. Also, lots of them have been given a make-over. Inside there is often an older building. The owner has chosen to pretend the house is Georgian by giving it a fine Georgian façade.

Above: Number 10, Castle Street, one of the finest houses along Castle Street, built by a wealthy corn merchant.

Choosing examples of wonderful Georgian architecture is difficult. You are spoilt for choice. Almost all the buildings along Castle Street, The Borough and West Street, are attractive. Number 10 Castle Street is certainly one. It was built by a wealthy grocer in about 1720. It is one of the few buildings on

Castle Street with a front garden. Number 44, called Guildford House, dates from the late eighteenth century. Its exuberant façade was added in the nineteenth century. The Nelson Arms is another fine building. Some say that Admiral Nelson's glass eye is embedded in one of its oak beams. Number 68 Castle Street has an interesting history. The workshop, and the yard behind it, is now home to Zizzi's, the pizza restaurant. In the past it has been a soft drinks factory, an ice rink and a delousing station for soldiers. For a while it was home to Farnham's tiny Castle Theatre.

On West Street, there are some wonderful Georgian houses. Wilmer House and Vernon House have already been mentioned. But look at Sandford House, or the group of houses numbers 88-94; number 88 is called Bethune House. Architects admire

these as perfect examples of Georgian architecture. Not all the buildings in Farnham are as old as they look. Farnham's great architect, Harold Falkner, liked rebuilding houses and making them look old. Many of the houses have been added to at different times. Number 40, for example: inside there are remains of an old house that was built in the mid fifteenth century. It was rebuilt in about 1660. Falkner added the front in 1910. The ancient-looking Bailiff's Hall is a

Above: West Street has many fine Georgian houses. This is one of the most 'perfect'.

wonderful reconstruction by Falkner of an old Tudor Building, but it actually dates from 1930.

If you look closely at such buildings, you often notice interesting details. Many have wall brackets which once held pub or shop signs. If you look at the walls carefully, you can see many bricked in windows. They were bricked in to avoid the brick tax. On Downing Street, you can see false windows. They look like windows but they are painted on. See if you can spot some. On Middle Church Lane you can see what are called 'mathematical tiles'. They look like bricks but are actually tiles made to look like bricks; another way of avoiding the brick tax.

Below: The heraldic crest of Farnham.

You can admire individual buildings in Farnham's Georgian centre, but most impressive is the overall effect. Each of the buildings is different, yet because they are in similar styles, they seem to fit together. The whole is greater than the sum of the parts.

Although Farnham prospered during the eighteenth century, fewer and fewer people were willing to be burgesses. The last burgess resigned in 1789 when he discovered that he had to pay for repairs to a bridge in Tilford. He walked up to the Castle and gave back to the Bishop the Borough Charter. Like the rest of Farnham, it became the responsibility of The Vestry.

See if you can:

- Decide what is your favourite Georgian house in Farnham.

- Find the mathematical tiles on Middle Church Lane.

- Spot two examples of 'blind windows', three examples of bricked in windows and four examples of old wall brackets.

Further reading:

The Town of Farnham. Four Volumes covering: A History of the Borough and Castle Street; Church Lanes, Downing Street and South of the River; West Street; and East Street, by Pat Heather, publ. by Farnham and District Museum Society, 2020.

The Nineteenth Century saw great change in Farnham. First of all, the population increased dramatically. Extra housing was needed. The workers' cottages along Loundes Way are a good example. They date from 1830. Some of the new houses were built with local bricks made from the clay that is found around Farnham. You can often tell that bricks are locally made because they have the imprints of birds or cats which walked across them as they dried. There is a cat's paw imprinted on a brick on Church Passage. See if you can find it.

Above: Loundes Passage where old artisanal houses are now highly desirable properties.

From the beginning of the Victorian Age, Farnham also started to grow outwards. First along east Street, with new housing built below Farnham Park. Then south of the River, where the old Firgrove and Waverley Estates were built over, and the grand houses of Great Austens laid down. Later still, a lot of development was carried out on the old hop fields north of West Street and Farnham grew westwards to where the Chantrys are now found. The westward development today only stops when you reach Coxbridge Farm.

During the nineteenth century, the roads around Farnham generally improved. For centuries most had been little better than mud tracks. Then someone had the bright idea of getting the people who used the most important roads to pay a 'toll' for using them. The money could then be used to keep them in good condition. These were called turnpike roads. The first were started in the eighteenth century

and they were added to in the nineteenth. They made travelling a little easier.

Two big nineteenth century developments changed Farnham even more than the turnpike roads. First the railway arrived at Farnham when the Station was built in 1849. Soon it was possible to reach Farnham from London. Wealthy gentry bought houses around, and in, Farnham so they could escape from smoky London at weekends. And people started living in Farnham and commuting to London. As hops declined towards the end of the nineteenth century, the wealth was replaced by what are called service industries, serving people with well paid jobs in London. To make it easy to get between the station and Farnham town centre, a new road, South Street was built.

The other big development was at Aldershot, which became the home of the British Army in 1853. Aldershot had been a small village and suddenly became a big town. Soldiers came to Farnham Station and got the coach to Aldershot. They brought their thirst with them and the number of pubs increased enormously.

Above: The Nelson Arms, another fine old building on Castle Street.

The Nineteenth Century was also a time of great reform. In the past, only the wealthiest had been able to vote. The great Reform Acts of 1832 and 1867 gave the vote to many more people. Farnham's greatest son, William Cobbett (1763-1835), who was born in the Jolly Farmer, spent his life fighting for reform and better conditions for the poor. He founded the Political Register to record exactly who said what in the House of Commons. It continues to this day and is called Hansard. Cobbett's Rural Rides is a classic, still worth reading. Cobbett's grave can be found in the churchyard of St. Andrews.

Our up-to-date Express from FARNHAM to GUILDFORD and back in one day (perhaps).

The authorities always had a problem knowing what to do with the poor, with people unable to work because they were sick or disabled. In Farnham, the old workhouse on Middle Church Lane was replaced by a new one. It was located on East Street where Farnham Hospital now stands. At the end of the nineteenth century, Farnham got another great writer concerned with the poor, though in his case it was with the rural poor. This was George Sturt whose family ran a wheelwright's business on East Street. His shop is still there. Living at the same time as George Sturt, William Willett, who came from Farnham, invented daylight-saving time.

Above: A postcard celebrating the Farnham to Guildford service. Reliability was clearly a concern then as now!

Public amenities also improved. Farnham got its own Gas Company, based south of East Street, and street lighting by gas. The Gas lamps on Castle Street date from 1834. Other amenities came later. By 1884 only slightly more than a quarter of the town's houses had a piped supply of water. Life expectancy in Farnham was poor. Many people died of cholera. Things improved dramatically after sewers were laid in the 1880s but lots of children stilled died of diphtheria, measles and scarlet fever until the twentieth century. Electricity had to wait until the twentieth century. In some of the villages around Farnham, electricity didn't arrive until after the Second World War.

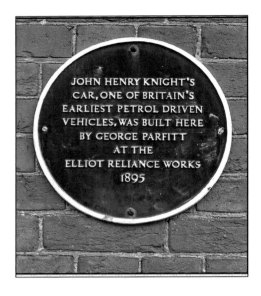

The Victorians always made sure that public buildings were handsome. They even made pump houses look like churches – there is a wonderful example surviving on Kimber Lane. See if you can find it.

Farnham got new industries during the Victorian Age. On 50 West Street, Parfitts made one of the first motor cars, designed by John Henry Knight in 1895. John Henry Knight also got one of the first motoring fines when his chauffeur drove down Castle Street without a man with a red flag walking in front. For a while Farnham had a factory making a car called The Pilgrim. On Ivy Lane there was a whalebone corset manufacturer in the 1890s. For nearly a hundred years from 1870, Crosby's was an important employer. After the war it made doors and Crosby's Doors were famous.

With all this change, the use of old buildings changed too. Shops came and went; houses became offices. Farnham Castle eventually became a Centre for International Briefing and then, more recently, a

Above: The plaque commemorating the building in Farnham of one of England's oldest cars, designed by John Henry Knight.

Below: The old United Reform Church, now the Spire Church; one of the most impressive of the many churches and chapels in Farnham.

wedding venue. The old Grammar School building on West Street became an art college. The clerical seminary on West Street became the Bishop's Mitre Hotel. Farnham even has two examples of public conveniences which were turned into houses: one on Park Row and one at 65A West Street. Just as the Church Vestry had taken over responsibilities from the Manor in the reign of Queen Elizabeth I, local government now took over the responsibilities from The Vestry. Local government built new amenities for the public. Sports grounds, schools and even a swimming baths beside the town hall. This was eventually closed and turned into a garden, Victoria Garden, on South Street. It is a hidden gem. See if you can find it.

For a long time, everyone went to church at St. Andrew's. But after the Civil War, lots of Christians didn't like the Church of England and set up their own churches. These were called non-conformist because they didn't conform to the rules and beliefs of the Church of England. Baptists, Methodists, Congregationalists ... lots of chapels were built. One of the finest, what is now called The Spire Church, you can find on South Street in 1873. It has a magnificent spire.

See if you can:

• Find the plaque celebrating John Henry Knight's motor car.

• Locate six religious buildings besides the church of St. Andrew's.

• See how many cat's and bird's footprints there are in the local brickwork.

Further reading:

Farnham Past, by Jean Parratt, publ. by Phillimore, 1999

Victorian Farnham, by B Ewbank-Smith, publ. by Phillimore, 1971

Farnham Buildings and People, by Nigel Temple, publ. by E W Langham, 1963, and Phillimore, 1973.

Opposite right: The Farnham Flame by Alan Collins, originally situated on the wall of the Woolmead, brings together the ancient themes of the flames of pottery kilns and the Bishop's mitre in a twentieth century design.

The Twentieth Century

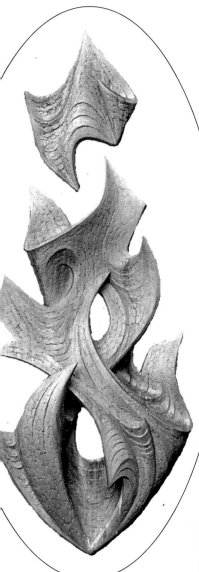

The twentieth century has seen even more change. Men from Farnham went off to fight in two world wars and many did not come back. Farnham made a special contribution to the first World War. It was in Farnham that the first two-minute silence was held, in 1916. You can see a blue plaque commemorating the event on the wall of Lloyds Bank on Castle Street. Bishop Talbot's sons went out to war as soldiers or chaplains. One of them, Gilbert, was killed and in his memory the servicemen's society, Toc-H was set up. During the Second World War, the secret Camouflage Training School at Farnham Castle helped develop new methods of camouflage.

There has been so much change, it is difficult to know what to mention. Most dramatic of all has been improvement in life expectancy. People can now expect to live to eighty years of age, twice what could be expected in the Victorian Age. All children now go to school. Farnham itself no longer has hops. Instead, it has shops. It has become a fashionable shopping centre. There have been some wonderful new developments, like the popular Lion and Lamb Yard, built where an old coaching inn used to stand. Other developments, like the Woolmead, recently demolished, proved less successful. The Art College has recently become the University of the

Creative Arts. Farnham has recently become a 'craft town'.

Of course, Farnham has its problems. Traffic has for a long time been one of them. To get cars away from the town centre, a bypass was built south of the town. It took many decades to complete. It unfortunately cut the town into two. But even this had a happy result. Building it meant creating a new roundabout at The Shepherd and Flock, one the biggest roundabouts in England. Inside the roundabout is a small hamlet where you suddenly discover what seems a lost world, a kind of time capsule in which the old Farnham survives.

People are again discussing what can be done about traffic in Farnham. When you walk around your town and think of its long history, you realise that things

Above: The ever popular Lion and Lamb Yard, a successful blend of old and new.

change utterly and some things don't change at all. Maybe that's the lesson history teaches us.

See if you can:

• Identify five buildings by Harold Falkner.

• Discover how to walk to Waverley Abbey from the Shepherd and Flock Roundabout.

• Work out why the eastbound carriageway on the Farnham bypass goes from two lane to one as you approach Hickley's Corner.

Further reading:

Harold Falkner – More than an Arts and Crafts Architect, by Sam Osmond, publ. by Phillimore, 2003

Edwardian Farnham, by B Ewbank-Smith, publ. by Charles Hammick, 1979

Above: The University of the Creative Arts.

Farnham in War and Peace, by B Ewbank-Smith, publ. by Phillimore, 1983

A Portrait of Farnham, by J Wood, publ. by Farnham Herald, 2003.

Farnham in the Great War, by Maurice Hewins, publ. by the Farnham and District Museum Society, 2020

Bond man	A man bound to do service without payment
Bond service	Service done without payment
Burgess	A freeman of a borough elected to govern the borough
Chancellor of England	In the Middle Ages, he was the manager of the King's household
Commutation	Replacement of bond service by a money payment
Demesne	A demesne was land retained by a lord of the manor for his own support.
Feudalism	A social system in which noblemen hold land from the Crown in exchange for military service, and the peasants live on their lord's land and give him bond service in exchange for protection.
Fine	A fee paid to the Manor Court
Freeman	A person who is not a serf or slave
Hundred	A subdivision of a county or shire, having its own court.
Magna Carta	The "Great Charter" guaranteeing English political liberties signed by King John in 2015
Malting	Converting grain into malt, used in making beer
Manor	A unit of medieval organization consisting of an estate under a lord enjoying a variety of rights over land and tenants including the right to hold a court.
Mesolithic	The Middle Stone Age before farming began about 4000 BC
Minster	An important church covering a large area. There was probably a minster in Saxon Farnham.
Neolithic	After farming had begun, about 4,000 BC
Parish	A small administrative district typically having its own church and a priest.
Serfdom	The condition in which a tenant farmer is bound to a plot of land and to the will of his landlord.
Tanyard	A place where skins and hides are tanned
Vestry	A group of parishioners responsible for the conduct of parish business.
Virgate	An area of land, usually about 30 acres in